First published by Fairy Thorn Press 2021

Newry

A catalogue record for this book is available from the British Library.

New Ireland on a Napkin: a political framework for the future

ISBN: 978-1-3999-0294-6

New Ireland on a Napkin

A political framework for the future

Francis Gallagher

Hello

Best Wishes,
Francis Gallagher

15/11/25

This book is about a better future for Ireland, through applying a system that has worked well in Switzerland.

I recognise the unique history and circumstances of Ireland and show how any alleviation of our problems should be anchored in our own experiences.

The case is presented for a confederal, unitary Ireland within a transformed EU, preventing the centralisation of power in the hands of a few.

These could be bankers, politicians, corporate executives, bureaucrats or any hierarchy that attempts to impose an institutional imperialism upon the people.

New Ireland on a Napkin presents a citizen's approach to politics, examining how we can achieve better government in Ireland through a participatory democracy.

A more co-operative, inclusive and civic way is required to build a New Ireland. This publication is about showing what this new way could look like.

My book is not a detailed policy and academic study of how a New Ireland could work.

This would be achieved through confidence building, consensus, peace and reconciliation.

Please let me know your vision for a New Ireland at
francispatrick.gallagher@ymail.com

The writings of the late Dr. John Robb, community surgeon and Irish Senator, 1982-89, were a great inspiration to me in writing this book. I have quoted directly from his works, with appreciation. John had a very advanced, yet grounded approach to politics that helped to develop my political awareness. Many of his ideas provide the philosophical backbone to New Ireland on a Napkin. Thank you John.

Thank you

Write it on a Napkin

"If you can't summarise your ideas for a New Ireland on Napkin, they are too complicated. Visualising in this way helps to inspire and make concepts understandable. There is no better way to achieve simplicity than seeing your thoughts taking shape on a napkin. Have a cappuccino at hand, which I like done 'old school' with plenty of chocolate on top.

Author

"Accountability should be the catch cry of all peaceful revolutionaries"

Dr. John Robb

Contents

CLIMATE CHANGE

I begin my book about climate change because if we don't solve this problem, everything else is academic.

We are facing a situation, probably for the first time in human history, that due to our planet overheating, the very existence of life on earth could be called into question.

I hope I am being alarmist because this means the situation can be retrieved.

A main cause of global warming is capitalism, both the western and Chinese state versions.

Capitalism is a very centrally controlled system that is reliant upon fossil fuels, especially for the transport of goods and international travel.

Professional scientific studies have shown that carbon emissions are destroying the earth's climate and leading us into other difficulties.

Journalists gave daily reports about how air travel spread the corona virus.[1]

Trade and travel around the world will exist in the future. But if our economic and political systems become more autonomous, local and self sufficient, travel will be less harmful to the environment.

Biodiversity

We should all wake up, smell the coffee and listen to what scientists are saying. There may be only 10 years to prevent a complete climatic crisis.

Those in positions of power have a duty, along with all of us, to act radically now to help heal a very ill planet.

Respecting biodiversity is one of the ways we can help to defuse the approaching disaster.

In their best selling book: *A Blueprint for Survival*, authors, Edward Goldsmith and Robert Allen wrote:

"The more diverse and complex the ego system, the more sustainable it is."

Each bee, bird, fish, animal, plant has a role to play in protecting our planet.

Variety is therefore a key component of life, so it makes sense that the same principle applies to our democracy: less centralisation, small is beautiful rather than big is better, decision making brought closer to the people.

Awareness of this point is important if we are to make progress, helping us to see that accountable government and the future of the earth are interdependent.

Micro water schemes could be one way to generate power in the future

Governments should be acting, not in terms of economic growth (GDP) but sustainable development, by planning capital projects that have a positive impact on the environment.[2]

We can all reduce our carbon footprint by making use of alternative, greener technologies.

Hydropower

In the 1990s, the late Seamus McDermott and I were invited by a local farmer to view the remains of an ancient irrigation duct. Seamus was from Newcastle in Co. Down.

The farmer had uncovered it beside a river that ran through his farm, just outside the above town and not far from Maghera village.

The find illustrated the long relationship local people had with water power and it made me think about its potential in a future Ireland.

The hydropower plants at Coolwood Nature Reserve in Killarney and Ardnacrusha in Co. Clare are modern day examples of how water power can be successful on our island.

Research should be carried out into the development of smaller hydro schemes for our towns and villages.

Californian Red Wood, Castlewellan Forest Park

Plant more trees

Thousands of years ago, Ireland was covered in ancient forests of oak, ash, birch, alder, willow, hazel, pine, yew and other species. Gradually, over time, these forests were diminished by human activity.

With the defeat of the Gaelic confederate forces at the battle of Kinsale in 1601, the island's land and trees were available for exploitation by the conquering English Tudor elite.

Eventually, much of the island's great forests were cleared to make way for a feudal landlord system and to provide timber for the construction of the royal navy's ships.

The tropical style woods that were once so prevalent in Ireland eventually became the fields we know today, enshrined in Westminster law by the Enclosures Act, 1750.

When I published this book in 2021, trees covered only 10% of Ireland's landmass but it should be increased to at least 30%. Farmers can be given financial support to grow trees.

The reforesting of Ireland would be a practical step toward reversing global warming. Trees absorb C02, are good for our health, alleviate flooding, improve drinking water and purify the air. So lets get planting.

A CONFEDERAL IRELAND

A Swiss friend once said to me that if his father in Switzerland wanted a pot hole in the road repaired, he would exclaim: 'I must call my civil servant'. [3]In a healthy democracy, this is the way it should be.

In a confederal Ireland, where accountability would go directly from government to the citizen, you should feel happy to contact a government official to get a public service issue sorted.

It would not be necessary for local politicians to exercise 'clout' because the system would be a lot more accountable and efficient.

Can we say this Swiss level of government accountability exists in Ireland or the UK today?

When we arrive at a point in Ireland, when we can speak like my Swiss friend's father, then we will have travelled a long way down the road to a New Ireland.

Sovereignty of the people

The confederal system enables public officials to respond more effectively to people's needs. It is based upon the idea that the people are sovereign and not politicians through parliament.

The UK and the Irish Republic's systems of government are representative democracies, whereas the Swiss democracy is participatory, in the sense the citizen has a direct influence over decisions. We need this in a New Ireland.

In a confederation, central government only retains the minimum amount of power and this is how the citizen is given more influence over policy.

In Switzerland, the democratic framework to help realise this are: village citizen assemblies, city municipalities, cantons and a confederal national assembly, in this sequence from the bottom up.

It's a grassroots democracy and it could work in Ireland because villages, townlands and cities could have citizen's assemblies while counties could be cantons.

Government would be more accountable to the citizen in a confederal Ireland

Co-operative government

A confederal Ireland would be a politically unified country although its government would not be very centralised.

Centralisation means that power is retained in the hands of a few politicians, civil servants, corporate executives and bankers. We can see why this has to be avoided.

Like Switzerland, Ireland could have a confederal assembly with 2 chambers, a national council and a council of states. The national council would have an executive of 7 people who are elected by its assembly who in turn are elected directly by the people.

The council of states would represent the cantons with each canton given seats proportional to its population. Fewer people would mean fewer seats.

In a confederation, there must be a majority in both houses (national council and council of states) for legislation to get through and one forum can compromise with the other.

Cantons have unicameral parliaments (single legislative chamber) and over 80% of all city municipalities and village districts could have a citizen's assembly, meeting in the town hall or village green.

Village Direct Democracy

Cantonal Parliaments

National Confederal Assembly

The national confederal assembly can also appoint the confederal court, military commander in chief and approve the annual budget, prepared by the 7 person confederal council.

This council meets 4 times a year for 3 weeks and is a collegiate body whereby all the 7 ministers take important decisions in co-operation and as a collective.

There is no prime minister thus ministers can be said to represent the diverse nature of Swiss society: religious, urban-rural, gender, language and identity aspects.

In a confederal system, the government is a coalition, making decisions by compromise and negotiation.

The seven ministers of the confederation form a permanent grand coalition. Seats are shared among parties according to their electoral strength and parties also co-operate in parliament.

SWITZERLAND

Confederal canton map of Switzerland

IRELAND

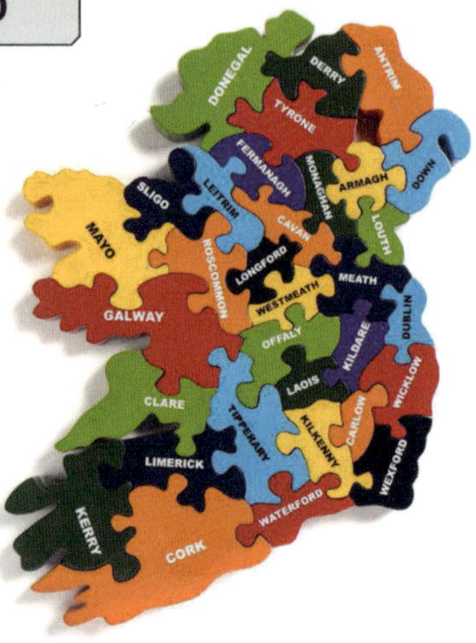

Confederal canton map of Ireland

Counties could be cantons

In the 1918 abortion referendum in the Irish republic, there was a majority vote in Donegal not to further liberalise abortion laws.

But because an overwhelming majority throughout the state voted the opposite to the pro-life majority in Donegal, the people of Donegal had to fall into line with the rest of the country.[4]

In a confederation, Donegal's decision would be respected by the state because Donegal would be a canton and its people would be sovereign.[5]

In the UK system of government, the Westminster parliament reserves the 'right' to over-ride decisions made by its regional assemblies.

This means the UK parliament could legally decide to dissolve the Scottish assembly, whereas in a confederation, there would have to be a consensus among the people of a canton for it to be disestablished.[6]

As we can see, a confederal government claims its legitimacy by focusing on achieving consensus among its citizens. It is probably the most progressive political system known to humanity and I think it would lead to the regeneration of Ireland.

DIRECT
DEMOCRACY

A confederation is a consensus-based system where everyone's views are respected and there is no need for a parliamentary 'opposition'.

The Westminster and Dail parliaments are adversarial with a government and opposition. It says to those people who have voted for parties that don't get into power – your views don't matter!

The author

Swiss Village

Direct Democracy

Direct democracy

Direct democracy is a vital part of a confederal system because the people can use popular initiatives to create or change policy.

Its designed to prevent government from placating people by giving the appearance of consultation that does not exist.[7]

Therefore its important that the citizen has a meaningful influence upon government decisions, otherwise one is not a citizen. This is why direct democracy is so important.

In a popular initiative, a series of choices can be presented to the public on a particular topic and they can vote in order of preference for each option.

This multi-option voting can be called a preferendum[8] and unlike a referendum, it seeks consensus rather than a black and white majoritarian decision. It would be ideal for Ireland due to the diversity of our people.

A citizen's initiative also allows the public to have a meaningful influence on laws before they are enacted. In representative democracies the public are 'consulted' on some legislation but this can be merely tokenism.

Direct democracy can be effective because senior government officials know the public can use the popular initiative if their views are being ignored.

Central confederal policy is therefore negotiated with the cantons, highlighting the healthy interdependence between all levels of government in Switzerland. [9]This is possible in Ireland too.

In a confederation, direct democracy takes place at 2 points, the citizen's initiative and citizen's assemblies.

In Switzerland, some Alpine villages practice the purest form of direct democracy called 'landsgemeinde': local people would assemble in their village square and make decisions by a show of hands.

At the time of writing, this was still carried out in Obwalden, Niwalden, Appenzell, and Glarus. In the rural area of Appenzell Inner Rhodes, on the last Sunday in April 2018, over 3000 people gathered to carry on this 600 year- old tradition. Decisions included agreeing money for a new hospital and banning fracking.[10]

I found it amusing, when a Swiss friend, who is very progressive in his politics, told a meeting at Newry that he would have more in common with a right wing politician in Switzerland than with most politicians in Ireland and the UK.[11]

This is because the Swiss political system is so much more advanced to what we have in these islands that this democratic DNA exists even within their more right wing parties.

Municipalities

In the Swiss confederation, municipalities and citizen assemblies are probably on a level to our local councils in Ireland but the Swiss version is much more accountable and democratic.

A Swiss municipality has a legal right to be and this cannot be changed by central government because in a confederation, power originates from the citizen.

Some Alpine municipalities have no more than a few hundred people but this is good.

How taxes are raised is central to the quality of local democracy in a confederation. Wolfe Linder wrote in his book, *The Swiss Political System*:

" The right to levy taxes and to decide the rates by themselves is the most important element in assuring the autonomy of local government."

In a New Ireland, the people could have the power to decide how money is raised and spent in their local area, so there will be an economic underwriting to municipal democracy. It will also help to spread economic development throughout the country, so it is not clustered around Dublin.

The enlarged size of Dublin today is mainly caused by the centralised nature of the Irish Republic's political system. In a confederation, economic

Ireland's new confederal parliament could be located at Athlone.

The Georgian parliament building has a lot of glass
to symbolise transparency

development is more balanced throughout the country because decision-making originates from the people in their locality or municipality.

Parliament location

If Ireland becomes a confederation, it will need a new parliament building. Why not site it at Athlone?[12] It is at the centre of Ireland and more convenient for people to attend. Symbolically this is important as a reassurance that most political and economic influence will not be centralised at Dublin.

A confederal parliament building, outside Dublin will be a clean start, sending out the crucial message, that the building of a New Ireland does not mean the South taking over the North by simply expanding the Dail.

Each canton could also have a parliament building and the public could choose its location. For example: the canton of Down could have its parliament at Ballynahinch, Downpatrick or Newtownards.

All parliament buildings in a confederation could make good use of glass to symbolise transparency of government. The parliament of Georgia, once a satellite state of the Soviet Union, is designed this way.

Confederal Constitution of Ireland

A confederal constitution for Ireland

The unity of Ireland means the unity of its people, so it could be argued that there is no legitimate right to claim Irish unity, if there is not a consensus for it among the whole people of Ireland.[13]

Problems arise when those who write a constitution, make a claim for a unity that does not exist among the broader community.

Such a document is irredentist in its make-up, with its authors viewing Ireland in terms of territory rather than its people.[14]

If we look at the constitution of Switzerland, it evolved over time, as Alpine communities asked to join the confederation because it was seen to be mutually beneficial.

The Swiss constitution therefore reflected a growing consensus and I would suggest this is how a new constitution for Ireland should develop.[15]

If sometime in the future, there is a border poll in Northern Ireland and lets say for discussion, 55% vote for unity and 45% support the status quo, it could be said that the question is not adequately resolved.

A New Ireland does not mean the absorption of the 6 northeastern counties by the southern 26 counties, because to coin a mathematical term, 6 into 26 'do not go'.[16]

The challenge therefore is to achieve consensus for a new constitution that would reflect the level of agreement for a particular model of government.

When this happens, it would be necessary to disestablish the present constitution of the Irish Republic and Government of Northern Ireland Act would no longer be necessary.

" A New constitution that would reflect in its articles, the degree of consensus which would be required to underline any claim to unity."

Dr. John Robb

New Ireland Forum. Report. 2 May 1984.

New Ireland Forum

It is crucial to understand that a New Ireland should not be about the North just joining up with the South, whereby there are a few amendments to the constitution of the 26 counties to accommodate Northern Ireland into the legal framework of an existing jurisdiction.

This would give the impression that the Irish Republic would be claiming the North in some way and this would not be a New Ireland.

A proposal was made that Northern Ireland's state boundaries and assembly could remain within a new all-island arrangement.[17]

In a genuine confederation, the people in the cantons are sovereign. If Northern Ireland was to become a semi-detached add on to the Irish Republic then all the people on the island would have an unaccountable political system.

The findings of the New Ireland Forum were published, 2nd May 1984. In its report, four constitutional frameworks were posed: the federal, confederal, unity state and joint Irish/British authority models.

But the first 3 options were incorrectly stated because they presuppose that the federal and confederal models are not unitary states when in fact they are. But they are not centralised unitary states.

The right way to list the options would have been: a

federal unitary state, a confederal unitary state and a centralised unitary state.

One could also read in the Forum report, the same idea mentioned above that as part of a confederal option, the jurisdiction of Northern Ireland would be intact (though separate from the UK) but be linked to the Irish Republic.

The reports authors may have understood this to be a confederation but it was really just a political conjunction because at its heart was identity and not accountability.

The Northern Ireland assembly would continue to be unanswerable to the public.

It is very clear that more research needs to go into the constitutional options that would be presented for future discussion.

The New Ireland Forum was very welcome because it opened up discussion about the form of a future constitution for the island.

Federalism

A federation is deceptive in that it subtly limits the citizen's influence by only delegating enough power in order to retain maximum power in the hands of a few.[18]

This is often done under the guise of decentralization. The citizen orientated, New Ireland person sees the solution in terms of autonomy or a confederal Ireland.

Dr. John Robb said that autonomy means taking back responsibility with insistence upon accountability.

He said autonomy has overtaken independence as the optimal state in self-determination: ourselves with or for others rather than ourselves alone should be mantra for creative survival.

The centralised model of government is the most autocratic because power is held by a coterie of politicians and corporate leaders.

The confederal system is the most progressive because it gives 'power to the people' to use a popular phrase.

Four Provinces

A four-province federation has been cited in some quarters as a future model of government for Ireland.[19]

This would entail having devolved parliaments in Ulster, Connacht, Leinster and Munster.

All four regional assemblies would send representatives to a federal council and there could be a national assembly elected directly from the people.

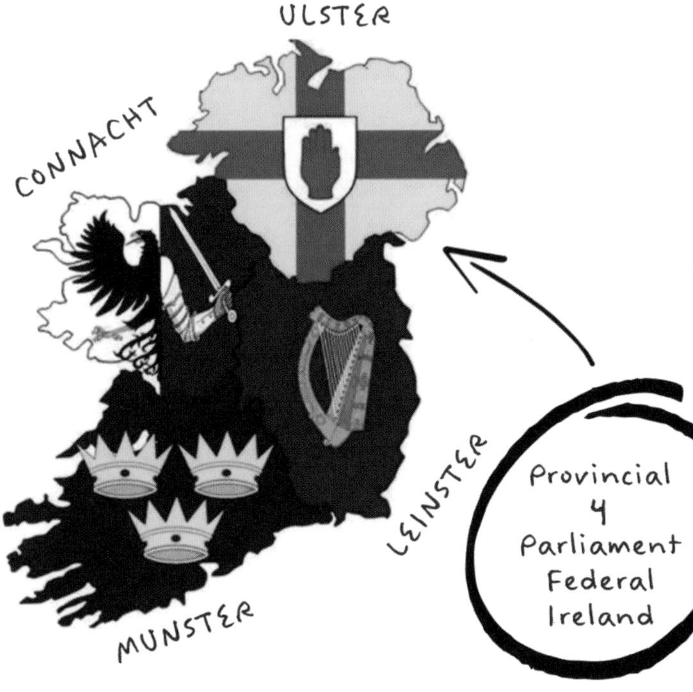

At face value, the four province federal option has got merit because it sounds more practical than having 32 county cantons. But 4 provincial parliaments could be as unaccountable as one that is centralised.

This could be the main problem with the four province federal system: power being devolved from central government rather than coming from the citizen.

In a confederation, the cantons and municipalities are sovereign through direct democracy. This is government by subsidiarity whereby central government only makes decisions where the public cannot at the grassroots.

So having 32 cantons in a New Ireland would bring power closer to the people than having 4 provincial parliaments. The 4 province federal model of government is worth further study.

Identity

In the New Ireland Forum report the federal and confederal models were presented as the same.

It was a very limited view of a confederal and federal constitution and if the issue of accountability in government had been addressed, a more imaginative confederal idea could have been offered.

If you wish to use the identity analysis to construct a confederal or federal framework in Ireland, it will be important to realise that the 'two traditions' in Northern Ireland (at the time of writing) are now nearly equal in numbers.

This could lead to the scenario where Northern Ireland is divided into two parts, with a 'unionist' and 'nationalist' majority in each segment, raising more problems.

Thus we can see the dangers of building government around identity rather than accountability. This is a fundamental flaw in the constitutional options presented in the New Ireland Forum report and in the Belfast/Good Friday Agreement.

Finances

Partition did not happen because of there being two separate religious and political identities in Ireland but because the wealthier Northern corporate elite did not want to get involved with the poorer south.

It was mainly down to what they viewed as a good business decision, downsizing from the unprofitable part of the company (the south) so to speak.[20]

The inaccuracies of the New Ireland Forum report have contributed to a lack of awareness over the years because many people have misunderstood the meaning of the constitutional options available to them.

It is remarkable how many people view the federal and confederal options as one when they are very different. The centralised unitary state was given as the preferred option of the New Ireland Forum but the accountability problems of a centralised government were not fully addressed.

"Before we start, I just want to let you know, I won't be changing my mind."

PLAN B

Economically, most people in Northern Ireland are worse off by being in the UK due to the limits of Britain's cash subvention. It is not enough to pay for full public services needed in a modern society.[21]

It is also true that a succession of elected officials in the Irish Republic have not met their obligations either. In a New Ireland, it does not have to be this way.[22]

Some people think that discussion is about persuading someone to change their mind and accept another idea. It is a very difficult thing to do because persuasion is an adversarial contest where one person gives ground to someone else's point of view.

Unionists have made their constitutional preference very clear and at this stage, many don't want to engage in discussions about a plan B to remaining within the UK. They don't want to take part in any discussions on this subject – period.

But if political and economic conditions change, which they always do, there may be more unionist people who may at least wish to look at alternatives.

This is in the sense that the vision of a New Ireland within a transformed EU is more attractive to remaining within the UK.

Discussion does not mean unionists would be negotiating a New Ireland but they would be considering their next desired option when and if they are ready to do so.

Agreement

New Irelanders may therefore discover that forging consensus with unionists for a confederal Ireland as a plan B is easier than trying to persuade them to break their constitutional link with the UK.

A plan B is not what some unionists may think, as a ploy to shunt them into a New Ireland. It is a genuine attempt to accept the unionist position without preconditions and to offer another option, should they want to consider it in the future.

Would it be possible for unionists to have dual membership of a confederal parliament in Ireland while attending Westminster too? This could pertain if the situation arose where a significant majority in the North wished to have a New Ireland.

Unionists may feel more confident knowing the variety of constitutional options available.

This is taking into account that there will be a large number of people in Northern Ireland who are very determined to stay within the UK in a scenario where, for example, a 55% majority vote to leave. A plan B may then become more relevant.

Europe

All life is interdependent in the sense that if someone is oppressed then we are in chains too. This is what is meant by the term 'freedom is indivisible'.[23]

Everyone wins when nations co-operate for the overall good. But there are those who hold the levers of power, for selfish reasons and only to benefit the few.

They centralise government, inequalities are sharpened and the environment is polluted.

This is why the people need to reassert their sovereignty by taking executive powers from these oligarchies.

Then give it to the many by founding participatory confederal democracies in their countries.

The challenge for the citizen is how to gain sovereignty, autonomy and self-determination, tempered by consensus, in a European society that has become more autocratic?

In their book: *The Swiss Miracle*, R. Benedikter and L. Kaelin wrote:

"Success in an interconnected world depends on blending integration with autonomy"

It means acting within a just union of interests by enhancing democracy where we live and work.[24]

The sovereignty of the people needs daily protection because it is one of the most precious things in the universe that could disappear without us noticing.

Transformed EU

Ideally, there would be a world of peoples, helping each other, with no borders. Forced emigration would belong to the past because there would be no wars of exploitation to drive people from their homelands.

But creating a better world order is very idealistic and maybe if we embrace the opportunity to achieve sovereignty of the people in Ireland, we will have taken a very important step toward a better Europe.

A positive vision would be a European council of sovereign confederal republics, working together for prosperity, peace and a healthy earth.

The Irish republic joined the European Economic Community in 1973, not as a subservient member, as was the case when Ireland was under the British Empire. For those who argue for Ireland to leave the EU, this is an important point.[25]

In the EEC, most power resided with Germany and France because their economies were the stronger, but Ireland was also moving forward.

EU central bank

Bankers

There are benefits of having unfettered access to EU markets, helping the Irish republic to become less reliant upon Britain.

Many people in Ireland worry about being dominated by the economic powerhouse of London and see the EU as a way out of this entrapment.[26]

This view has coloured public opinion in Ireland so much that the control of Brussels is preferred to the control of London, despite both undermining Ireland.

A banker once said: 'Give me control of your money and I will have control of your country.'[27] Are both jurisdictions in Ireland controlled by banks in another country?

A New Ireland would not have enough influence to change the EU, so it would be astute to wait and see what the other stronger nations do. If their economies go into decline, then there could well be progress toward a more democratic EU.

Regions or autonomies

I hope this could be a Europe of autonomies instead of regions because the latter are diminished territories[28] whereas the former are more democratic, vibrant and prosperous.

It could be argued that the US, Britain and the European banks should finance the transitioning of the both states in Ireland into a New Ireland.

This is in the hope that the people on the island could hopefully become members of a restructured, more democratic EU.

The political and humanitarian crisis in the oil rich Latin American state of Venezuela illustrates inconvenient questions for supporters of the EU as currently constituted.

On the 5th February 2019, it was reported that Britain, Germany and Spain were among 15 European nations supporting US attempts to overthrow the socialist government of Venezuela and the US embargo of the country.[29]

What is the type of EU that can support such aggression against a sovereign nation and what type of Ireland are we to be part of a centralised EU capable of such a policy?

Corona virus

It seems that the corona virus was allowed into Ireland in March 2020 because the Irish government refused to health check passengers coming into Dublin airport from Northern Italy.[30]

Some people argued that flights to Northern Italy from Ireland should not have been allowed at such a critical time but amazingly they continued.

Irish government officials stated that restrictions on travellers would not be effective in stopping the virus because infected people would come into Ireland from other destinations.[31]

But this argument does not stand up to scrutiny because the audit trail of travellers can be easily checked at any port before entry is allowed.

It appears that the initial cases of corona virus came into Ireland unhindered from Northern Italy and through Dublin airport, just before the other European states stopped international tourist travel.

So the question needs to be asked: why was the Irish government so slow to act when we were still in what could have been the preventative phase?

Was it sheer arrogance and incompetence or did the EU direct the Taoiseach not to interfere with freedom of movement?

It is highly likely that Ireland would have been free from corona virus if both governments on the island had acted quicker.

There was also the added spectacle of empty planes flown to European destinations in order to keep airport landing places, the result of a EU directive.

Although linked to wider globalisation of the economy, we had the lunacy of medical personal protective equipment having to be ordered from China when it could have been made locally.

There was not enough corona virus testing kits in Ireland when they could have been manufactured here with the right organisation in place.

The corona virus crisis certainly highlights the need for more autonomy and subsidiarity for nations within the EU, to act independently, when required.

Subsidiarity of government means power is brought closer to the people, so in a European context, Brussels would leave most policy decision-making to the citizen.[32]

This was how the EU was intended to be by its founders, before it became centralised and bureaucratic.

Ireland is not Germany or France and what is good for these countries is not always good for Ireland.

Yellow vests

There is no doubt the EU needs to change and there may come a point when those who control it, will have to agree to a restructuring of the EU system in order to prevent other countries from leaving.

There is much frustration among citizens, partly caused by the dysfunction of the banking system that contributed to the policy of austerity.

During the yellow vest protests in Paris of December 2018, a citizen said on TV: 'what we need is another French revolution to show the people still have power'.[33]

The author of this book supports gradual peaceful change but I use the above quote to show the frustration many people have with not feeling democracy where they live and work.

Noam Chomsky said if the EU states kept their individual currencies, they could devalue and export their economies out of recession. A common EU interest rate does not work because each member state's economy is different.

A pragmatic way to transform the EU would be by progressive movements first democratising the nation state. This would entail having confederal, participatory democracies at a national level as a precursor to making EU institutions more accountable.

"PEOPLE STILL
HAVE POWER!"

It would be difficult to have a pan European democratic movement, attempting to transcend the national representative democracies, in order to create a new EU. There is no harm in trying but logistically it would be very overwhelming.

But hey: why not try?

POLITICAL CAREERISM

Political careerism means the attainment of political office to further one's own political career rather than to improve society.

There are politicians who see their role merely as a job and are bound by few ideals.

Political careerism is a disease that destroys democracies because it's a behaviour that hollows out the core of a good democracy, leaving an unaccountable, empty shell.

It has fed into the general disillusionment among the public for many politicians and our remote political institutions in general.[34]

This feeling of alienation reflects a deeper sense of powerlessness in Ireland, the UK and in many other countries.

Many people are frustrated with decisions about their future being made by unaccountable politicians and corporate executives.

Politics is too important to leave to the politicians and this is why we need a confederal system to include people more in the decision making process.

If this does not happen, there is a danger that fascism could raise its ugly head again and usurp the power of the citizen by using their marginalisation to gain control of the state.[35]

Advice from tone

The United Irish leader, Theobald Wolfe Tone, conveyed this dilemma of politics, power and corruption well in a letter from Philadelphia, 1st September 1795, to his friend Tom Russell in Belfast:

'Power long exercised would corrupt an Angel'[36] Tone wrote. How right he was.

Another problem engendered by political careerism is that it has a tendency to make politicians state not what they believe to be true but what will advance their opportunity for promotion within the party or government.

Many career politicians are like magpies: they pick up other people's good ideas, use the labelling but don't implement the substance.

As a result, those who are genuine about change will find it difficult to get the public to support a radical proposal because career politicians have misrepresented it.

For example: many politicians now realise their game is up and that people are fed up with their antics.

To circumvent this, they hijack the language of progressives who want to create a better politics. So many politicians say 'we want a new politics' when they actually mean continuing with their old habits.

This is why political careerism is like a virus because it mutates, reinventing itself to try and fool the people. The only way to cure this disease is by increasing political awareness.

Political partyism

Some modern day political parties are run like corporations and are autocratic in how people are selected to run for elections.

Career politicians will not speak out against the party because this is viewed as detrimental to their career prospects, especially when the party whip is applied.

The result can be a public not properly informed by their political representatives and in some cases, the promotion of a type of politician lacking the backbone and integrity to say and do the right thing.

These are not the type of people you want to have in positions of political authority but our current system of unaccountable representative democracy encourages their advancement.

Theobald Wolfe-Tone

How can we overcome this scourge of political careerism?

The first step is to have political parties where members genuinely select their leaders and those who run for office.

Quite often lip service is given to this principle, with party nominations handed down through families from parents to their children, nephews and nieces – the worst type of nepotism.

Therefore, it makes sense to get people into office and government whose primary concern is to improve the country. With a little bit of effort, these people can be spotted and nurtured.

Voluntary ethos

The part-time and voluntary ethos in government can help too because some people who own a business or have a well-paid professional job, may not need a parliamentary salary.

They could bring their expertise to bear upon decisions if they were ministers.

How many times has there been a minister of health who does not know what a good health service should look like?

A basic living wage and expenses, enshrined in law, should be paid to political representatives who don't have an income outside of their political work.

A decline in political careerism would be an immense improvement of our political system.

There are those who will say that people with ability will not contribute to government without a good salary. A country would be better off not having these people in office because professional knowledge without a vocation is a poor combination.

In Switzerland, the voluntary and part-time principle has served them well in politics.[37] The confederal system discourages political careerism.

Lets support politicians who are motivated to act according to their ideals rather than the party line.

Constitutional options

In order to move the political economy of Ireland forward, it will be necessary to consider alternative constitutional options to the status quo. Here are a few:

- A confederation of these islands brought about by the succession of Scotland from the UK. A parliament could be in the Isle of Man

Swiss parliament in session

Swiss parliament building

and representatives would attend from Wales, Ireland, Scotland and England (WISE).38 All would have equal decision powers, backed up by a transformed EU.

- Confederal, sovereign, unitary Ireland within a council of European sovereign republics.

- Confederal, unitary Ireland that is not a member the EU but has bilateral trading treaties with it. Similar to the Swiss arrangement with the EU.

The most attractive of these options for Unionists, as an alternative to the current constitutional arrangements, would probably be the confederation of the Isles.

Would it be possible for unionists to retain their link with England, Scotland and Wales while also playing a role within a confederal Ireland?

Neutrality

A country's political and military neutrality is important for its people to be free and happy and the Swiss are a shining example of this.

Over the centuries, they largely managed to stay neutral in Europe's conflicts and the Swiss economy prospered as a result.

Neutrality does not mean Ireland would turn the other way from helping a people under imperialist aggression.

It would entail not taking part in imperialist wars of aggression and without this policy an Ireland worth building cannot be achieved.

Neutrality needs defending so Ireland would need to have a good navy and citizen defence.

Neutrality is the most powerful argument not to be part of a centralised European political system. Such an autocratic EU would inevitably lead to the formation of a European military power that could become imperialist in the future.

Non -alignment is not neutrality,[39] so for example, the Irish Republic, by allowing US rendition flights (in its war with Iraq) through Shannon airport was not acting as neutral state but as a non-aligned one. This was because it was supporting the US military operations by facilitating its planes at Shannon.

ECONOMY

I am lucky in life to meet creative people who have helped me to think about the study of history.[40]

By listening and taking on board their views, I have learnt that economics is a major influence upon political change.[41]

Economics will probably decide the future of Northern Ireland (although its people should do this).

This is because it is costing the city of London billions of pounds each year and Whitehall may be looking for ways to off load this money-losing subsidiary (NI).

The Irish Republic does not wish to 'buy it over' so to speak, because Northern Ireland is being financed by another corporation: London.[42]

Swiss clock

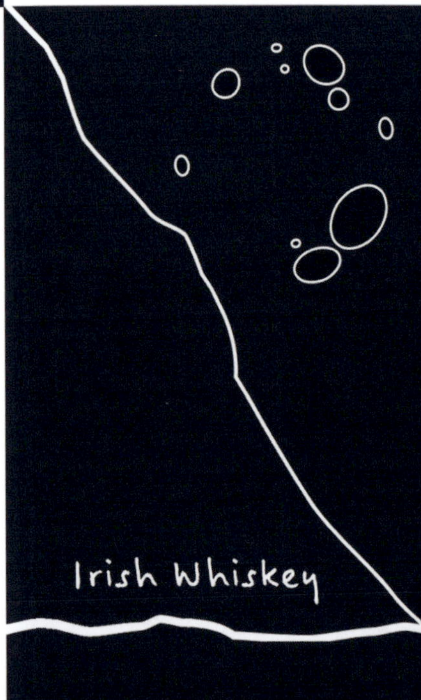
Irish Whiskey

What is wealth?

In trying to imagine and chart a course for a healthy new-Ireland economy, one has to apply the common-sense of the accountant or shopkeeper.

In both professions, prosperity is a matter of credit and debit. The former representing the wealth generated and the latter, the money spent.

This may sound simplistic but many economists use too much jargon and over complicate economics. Is it not a subject mainly about understanding money, wealth and how they differ?

Cash is different from wealth because money is made from paper and metal, whereas wealth is the skills and knowledge of people.

With the advance of on-line banking, some argue that paper money and coins will become obsolete, as we can make transactions by using our debit card.

But this could be premature because the corona virus has taught us the vulnerability of capitalism and the importance of having local control, including cash in your hand.

The materials that make up money are valueless but its power lies in its exchange value, underwritten by the banks and government.

The powers that be name a currency and give it an exchange value. This was seen as a step forward from the days when people bartered to get the things they needed.

A country's wealth, therefore, is its people who are developed through the quality of their education and political institutions.[43]

Money is the oil that lubricates the moving parts of an economy, so it is important that a country has control of its money supply, to have sustained prosperity.

If future governments in Ireland developed the skills and knowledge of the people, to a much greater extent than is happening today, more wealth would be created by the production of quality indigenous products for export.

Ideally, exports should surpass imports, generating capital for investment in Ireland.

Confederal political economy

It makes sense to argue that the very first task to be completed in building a New Ireland economy is to radically change our political institutions to make them more accountable.[44]

The next step will be to equip people with the intellectual and manual skills to encourage business innovation to create products that will be the best in the world.

As we can see, the Swiss have done this by implementing the above reforms and with few of their own raw materials, can produce products that are unsurpassed in the world economy.

This is why, like Switzerland, Ireland's political economy should be confederal because it is the best political framework to produce accountability and prosperity.[45]

In Ireland, prosperity is relative for those who have and have not. But how long will the good times last for those doing well in a country with such high levels of debt?

We are vulnerable without the solid foundations of a robust home industry.

How long will the current EU finances (in the South of Ireland) and multi-national tax returns last to keep the ship afloat?[46]

Newry City could be a municipality in a confederal Ireland

Innovation

By innovation and new home-grown businesses, prosperity can become more sustainable but it is vital to manage it through a fair taxation system.

In a confederal Ireland, taxation should be viewed as a necessary requirement to improve our well-being rather than as a burden upon the people.

In a confederation, each municipality and canton would raise taxes locally to be spent locally.[47] This would go beyond the current rates levying powers local councils have today but local government (municipalities) would be more accountable to the people.

But there is less likelihood of malpractice because major projects and policy applied at local level will have achieved community consensus through the confederal system of direct democracy.

For example: Newry could be a municipality within the canton of South Down with ratepayers having a say on how to raise taxes and how they are spent.

Fairer taxation

The 3 levels of the confederal government can raise direct taxes on income and profit. Central government can raise VAT with some taxation on consumption and stamp tax. Fees for bin collection and other direct tax is a feature of municipal government.

This system of local grassroots municipal taxation should have the support of the people and no major project could be undertaken without their consent.

In a New Ireland, richer cantons can help to finance poorer cantons. Money is raised where money is spent in the canton system.

It is inconceivable in the confederal system that forums of the people decide how to spend money but not how to raise it.

In a confederal Ireland, the distribution of money derived from taxation could be as follows: 40% for the municipalities, 44% for the cantons and 16% for the confederal state.

The confederal economic system is about developing the abilities of everyone whereas the more centralised state is designed to control people by not developing their talents to the full:

"As a rule, each level of state receives the taxes it raises"

Wolfe Linder

“Because it is easier for centralist systems to control societies that only develop a small fraction of each individual’s resourcefulness”

Dr. John Robb
New Ireland: sell out or opportunity

Bulmer Hobson

Bulmer Hobson highlighted the importance of having control of your currency. He wrote in *Ireland, Yesterday and Tomorrow* (c1968):

> "I am of the opinion that the external value of the Irish currency should not be held arbitrarily at any level which may be determined by circumstances in another country: but should be determined by the purchasing power in Ireland."

This means that the value of Ireland's money should not be determined by forces outside of the people of Ireland or put another way, the German central bank should not have control over our currency.

An economic development commission would be

tasked with designing public projects, by consent, for a sustainable native economy. It would be done by working in partnership with the currency commission within a broad governmental economic and monetary policy.[48]

Is it not better to pay people a fair income to contribute to the economy than a paltry unemployment benefit to be unproductive? Good jobs can be created if the will is there.

Sustainable economic success (instead of the boom-bust cycle we have now) is more likely to be achieved in a confederal Ireland.

In turn, it will be easier to develop a highly qualified workforce, stable banking, local manufacturing and tourism. As a result, the exports of luxury goods will increase.

Ireland should be able to produce a lot of its own food. Most exports will go to the UK and EU with much employment provided by small to medium sized business (SMEs).

Economies of scale

It's easier to create a good quality of life and economic prosperity in a smaller country, with fewer people than it is in a large one that is over populated.

In the near future, the whole of Ireland could have a population of over 7 million. It would therefore be easier to cater for their needs than it is for the population of England that is over 54 million at the time of writing this book.

Credit Union: a good role model

The environment and economy should be interdependent because economies are damaged by an obsession with growth at the expense of the environment.[49]

More money is required to undo harm done to our natural assets, which if left polluted, will affect jobs in tourism and service industries.

There should be a clear distinction between economic growth and economic development. The latter improves the overall quality of life for everyone but the former measures success by a rise in GDP, creating more inequalities.[50]

Ireland, while under the control of London, for centuries, paid more (in proportion to its size) than Britain in taxes.[51] Ireland is therefore owed a very substantial tax rebate from Britain's exchequer that could help meet the pension cash needed when transitioning to a New Ireland.

Agriculture

Future food production in a New Ireland should be produced in a more sustainable way because our current system of industrial agriculture disconnects farmers from the land and destroys much of the natural habitat.

Rural communities are in decline on the Emerald Isle and have been for many years. Take a walk through Ireland's countryside today and you get a feeling of emptiness, lack of vibrancy, loneliness.

Where are the farm workers bringing in the harvest and looking after the cattle?

What has happened to the wildlife: wasps, bees, corncrakes, rabbits, foxes, ladybirds, kingfishers, greenfinches were once a common site in my childhood but not now.[52]

Ireland used to be covered with clean rivers, abundant with fresh water trout, but there are fewer now. I remember catching fish as a child with a fishing line rapped around a stick.

Much of this beauty has been decimated by an excessive reliance on modern farming techniques and the application of a EU common agricultural policy (CAP). It discouraged innovation and competitiveness, treating all countries with uniformity.

CAP has been weapon of mass destruction to

farming in Ireland and in third world countries.

Over 50% of all CAP payments in 2015 went to just 12% of farmers in the Irish republic.[53] There needs to be a ceiling for the amount of payments given out to one individual and smaller farmers should be given a fairer proportion of CAP payments.

The key point is that subsidies should reward sustainable, environmentally friendly farming. The Swiss do this with great success.[54]

In Ireland we are in a different situation: EU subsidies have become an end in itself. It is understandable that many farmers have become reliant upon them but we need to recognise that the EU might not be able to continue making these payments.

Further reform of CAP is needed so it responds to the individual needs of each country.

It is very difficult for small farmers to survive in Ireland, yet they were once the backbone of our island society, living a life that was tough but good in many ways too. So give farmers a say on designing agricultural policies.

The corona virus plague made me realise how easily the global system of importing food could break down. Since very few of us know how to cultivate crops, we would be in big trouble.

Cultivating skills should be taught to the public with land set aside in every school, town, village, city and farm to grow organic food.

Home grown is good not only for food but in democracy and manufacturing too. It will mean the difference between surviving and perishing.

In the New Ireland, organic farming should be encouraged and the use of pesticides on non-organic farms should have stricter controls.

Like the Swiss, we should allow third world agricultural produce into our island, tariff free.[55] I hope in the future there will be no third world but equality of opportunity for everyone.

Eat less meat

Many cattle feeds contain soya but animal habitats are destroyed throughout the world to grow soya, which can be genetically modified.

The Swiss have banned the use of GM feed for animals and this is part of their constitution,[56] so why has the Irish republic not moved in this direction? Too much of our land is given over to grazing rather than tillage.

There is no reason why we can't grow animal feed in Ireland by developing alternatives. In a New Ireland, we should eat less meat, grow most of our animal feed and thus make sure it is GM free. We will be healthier as a result.

Food sovereignty should be the key phrase: this means our food should be sustainable, diversified, local, organic, GM free with more emphasis on creating jobs in farming with good salaries.

Fishing

The sad fact is that much of our sea fish harvest has been seriously depleted and a lot of our fresh water stocks suffer from pollution.

Ireland's past is interlinked with its waterways and the fishing industry is very much a part of who we are and should be protected from over exploitation.

The Irish republic's fishing industry has not faired well from the EU with industrial sized fishing trawlers from other countries exhausting our fish stock.

This is partly the result of a deal done for the Irish republic to enter the EU in exchange for subsidies.[57] It has greatly diminished Ireland's fishing industry, leading to the decline of coastal fishing towns.

You could argue a whole industry and its skills were traded for EU subsidies, money that could be withdrawn by Brussels anyway. But this too needs to be weighed up with the overall benefit of Ireland being part of the EU.

Just before EU membership, the people of Ireland had access to one of the richest stocks of fish in the world. For a 50 miles radius around the island's coast, fishermen/women had free and exclusive access to this fishing.

Associated skills are being lost, making it more difficult to fish our waters again in the future if survival requires it.

Ireland's fishing industry will have to be replenished by having more control of who fishes our waters.[58] This brings us back to the need to transform the EU from how it is currently constituted.

Management culture

A vital part of building a confederal political economy in Ireland will be to foster a more positive public sector management culture, where needed.

Although it is not all bad, irregular results and legal investigations[59] have highlighted regressive management practices in parts of today's public administration here.

Poor management is more prevalent in countries with unaccountable political systems, giving rise to inefficient government departments. Unfortunately, Ireland is one of these places.

In this environment, it is more likely that people with negative 'management' attitudes will be promoted because they tend not to challenge a dysfunctional system, especially one where they have benefited.

Promotion boards can use pseudo objective interview techniques to give a veneer of objectivity to a process that is prone to individual bias. This is especially so, if those interviewing a candidate already know the interviewee, which is more common than you think.

In many offices, bullying, division and low achievement can be the outcome.[60]

The public service attracts quite a few people in authority who are not team players and who don't have the welfare of their staff and society at heart.

In Ireland's public sector, much of the management practice focuses upon managing impressions[61] rather than delivering a good service.

What tends to happen, all too often (although not always) is that people are promoted who don't have the necessary discursive and analytical thinking skills to develop people and an organisation.

A friend described this phenomenon as 'institutional imperialism'[62] because in these organisations, dialogue is stifled, so the culture is anti-dialogical. Many people are promoted (though not all) to keep this status quo intact.

I would suggest that government departments therefore need to be restructured along participatory decision making lines, giving employees a genuine influence upon operational and policy decisions.

This is infinitely better to the memos down and information up, statistics driven approach that exists in much of Ireland's public administration today.

It is common in very hierarchical bodies such as the public service and poses the question: are government departmental statistics manipulated to give an impression that targets and results are being achieved?

There is no point 'reaching the target if you miss the point', which is working as a team to genuinely help people.

Excessive bureaucracy is the big enemy, symptomatic of a poisoned body politic, giving rise to the above problems.

In a New Ireland, government departments will be made more accountable if they are integral to the confederal framework of the country.

A delightful reward will be a new type of public administration that is open to critical thinking with fewer petty bureaucratic functionaries in positions of authority.

It may be necessary to restructure large government departments into smaller, more autonomous, non – hierarchical teams, to promote this creativity. It works well in the world of business whereby large corporations are reorganised into smaller companies.[63]

It could be argued that this transformation of public sector management is required, if we are to grow a vibrant New Ireland economy.

Infrastructure

Rail travel should be encouraged because it is more environmentally friendly. This will mean investing in a new, more extensive, high-speed rail network for the country.

People and freight can be transported by rail a lot quicker and safer. Railways are easier and cheaper to construct than roads. This form of transport needs to be less costly for passengers.

In a new more accessible railway system, it should not cost more than £5 for a return ticket from Newry to Dublin. A new island wide railway service should be step on, step off, safe, luxurious, regular and cheap. As in days gone by, the rail network should extend to towns and villages.

Within a confederal Ireland, because the cantons will have more autonomy, more products will be produced locally which is good for the environment, cutting transport costs.

A vital part of our infrastructure will relate to tourism and this is why our inland waterways should be further developed.

At Newry in 1741, work commenced on the first summit canal on these islands.[64] Its city section is in fairly good condition although the inland stretch is not.

All of Ireland's canals should be reconnected and most certainly the Newry-Portadown canal should be reopened to Carlingford Lough.

It would be central to the regeneration of Newry, linking up with the Ulster canal and the island wide inland waterways network. Our canals should be respected by keeping them clear of overhead structures.

Many business executives, especially from foreign companies, like to live beside waterways because they are interested in boating.

It's a no brainer to protect and make full use of our waterways and when we consider they were dug out with picks and shovels in the 18th and 19th centuries, there is no reason why, with modern technology, they can't be developed today.

Photoshopped image of a re-opened Newry Canal

Globalisation

We need to dispel the idea that globalisation is free trade as two thirds of the world's trade is in dollars.[65]

The Federal Reserve greatly influences global monetary and trade policies and globalisation is mainly controlled by the US. At the time of writing this book, the richest 1% of the world's population owned 46% of global money.[66]

Globalisation is a propaganda term to give the impression there is a global economy to help everyone. In fact it means an economic system designed specifically to benefit the United States multi-national corporations.

US capitalists use globalisation, through a policy of neo-liberalism, to open up, deregulate and control the economies of other countries.

Third world countries, such as the Congo, are exploited to supply the West with cheap minerals to make computers and mobile phones.[67]

The printing of cheap money and credit is a weapon of globalisation that can be used to create indebtedness among smaller countries, undermining their democracy.

The world- bank, international monetary fund and EU central bank, use austerity economics and poor public services to pay for these policies.

They control the creation and flow of a lot of the world's money and at the centre of this is the bank of international settlement, the central bank of all central banks.

Globalisation is the new imperialism but instead of sending a gun- boat up Dublin's river Liffey, the panzers across Europe or troops to Vietnam, the World Bank and International Monetary fund is deployed.

The people of Ireland need to ask themselves do they want to be part of a system that enslaves large parts of humanity and is destroying the planet?

The alternative is to make sure we have control over what at least Ireland does and to plan properly to change the world.

The answer to globalisation is mass, peaceful, popular movements that build awareness for direct democracy.

Utopian, I know, but its better to aim high in life.

Immigration

Switzerland is a fine example of how controlled immigration can be a blessing.

After the 1572 St. Bartholomew's Day massacre in Paris, thousands of French Protestant Huguenots fled to the Swiss Alps.

They brought their famous watch making skills, flair for trade and entrepreneurialism. Trade did not require much capital but mainly the ability to network and to work hard.

The Huguenots were the founders of the Swiss private banks and watch industry, skills that helped develop their engineering sector too.[68]

The important point to make is that immigration is essential for a country's development provided the immigrants are offering needed skills and labour.

James Breiding, writing about immigrants coming to Switzerland, states in his wonderful book, *Swiss Made: the story behind Switzerland's Success* :

" Immigrants are potential agents of industrialisation, because the only way to climb the social ladder is through achievement, with few around to lend a helping hand."

Population

Ireland needs more skilled people from abroad because the country has too few people to be sustainable. More doctors, nurses, engineers, financiers would be a great boost.[69]

The overall population of Ireland (at the time of writing) is approximately 6.6 million.[70] A lot fewer people than is needed if our economy is to develop, but too many people on a small island would not be good either.

It is important that an Ireland of the future provides a refuge for the politically persecuted and we could be a leader in this field.

Many newcomers to Ireland, over hundreds of years, became an important part of the Irish nation and it could be argued, our distant ancestors were once immigrants too.

It is also true that the number of people living in a future Ireland should be planned rather than determined by outside forces. An over populated island would diminish the quality of life for everyone, which is the case in England.

In a new non-imperialistic world, there should be no need for mass emigration, as most people prefer to live on their own land, if given the right opportunities.

Healthcare

The ideal for a caring and efficient health care provision would be based upon what I call the Egyptian pyramid model.

This means that the maximum amount of health care possible is provided at the lowest grassroots level.

An acute hospital is not the best place for a patient to stay for long periods due to the risk of infection and declining spirits.

With the pyramid approach, it would be envisaged that most consultations and treatments could be given in the community: the patient's home, GP surgery and district health hub. Obviously there will be instances where someone will need care in a local acute hospital.

Dr. John Robb argued in his seminal publication: *Long live the small acute hospital*, that over 80% of general acute care can be carried out in the small, local acute hospital. The remaining 20% of patients would require super specialist care in a central location.

But with advances in medical technology, much specialist treatment can also be given in the community too, such as advanced elective care in a local health hub.

But it is also recognised that some specialist doctors need to be located at one central location, but there is an obsession with training specialist doctors to the

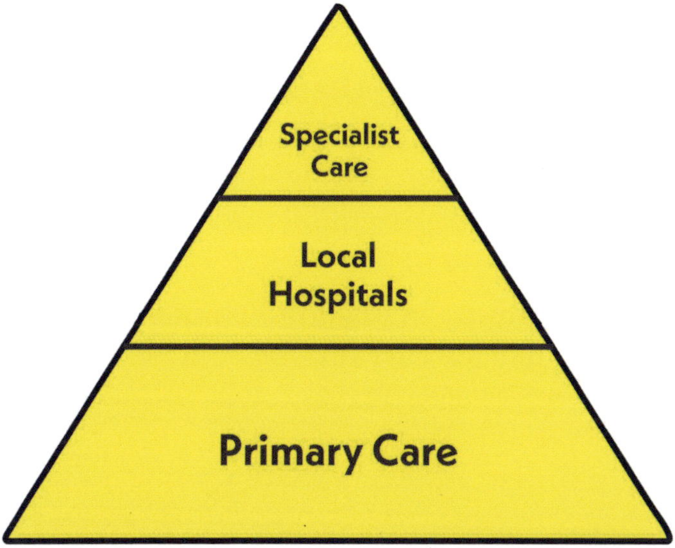

New Downe Hospital

extent that there seems to be one for every part of the human body.[71]

This can lead to a gathering of specialists in one big 'centre of excellence' assuming that excellence can only take place at the centre.[72]

It may not always be right to view the big hospital as the nirvana of acute care but the controllers of modern medicine would have us believe the myth that big is better.

More general surgeons need to be trained to cater for the larger numbers of people requiring their skills and they could be renamed 'community surgeons'.[73]

The pyramid model of health care can be explained as follows: the base and largest part of this structure covers primary and acute care in the community. The middle to upper torso represents general acute care in the local acute hospital and the top of the pyramid shows the proportion of health care usually needed for super specialist treatments.[74]

Governance

In terms of health care governance, in a confederal Ireland, the people, through their canton, would control the provision of health care.

This is the opposite to what pertains now in Ireland where health care is controlled by a centralised department of health.

In a New Ireland, hospitals would be governed by a forum of medical and nursing staff, along with other workers and members of the public.[75]

They would be responsible for managing the hospital and its budget, allocated by the canton's government.

This would take overall control away from the health service managers, cutting down on red tape, incompetence and wastage of resources.

It would be a public funded health service free at the point of use. Many more doctors and nurses would be trained and our health service would be so good that staff retention would not be a problem.

Like Cuba, Ireland could have an international medical service for doctors who wished to work abroad in disadvantaged countries. One of the measures of our success would be how well the most vulnerable patients are treated.[76]

Education

Patrick Pearse wrote in *The Murder Machine* how important it is for children to have an inspiring teacher and freedom to learn.

His views on education are very progressive and could still be of great help to the people of Ireland in the future.

Pearse founded a school, St. Enda's, in 1908, at Ranelagh, Dublin. In 1910, it moved to a substantial Georgian house at Rathfarnham, an historic part of the city.

It was once the home of the famous Emmet family, with Thomas Addis and his younger brother Robert, leaders in the United Irish movements of 1798 and 1803.

Robert strolled along the gardens of his Rathfarnham home with Sarah Curran and this helped to inspire Pearse to locate his school there.[77]

Robert Emmet was executed by the authorities for his attempt to organise a rising in 1803.

St. Enda's school at Rathfarnham, Dublin

Freedom to learn

Pearse had great hopes for St. Enda's and it was to be a positive setting to enable young people to learn.

Considering the centralised control of schools today and in Pearse's time, St. Enda's pupils had a remarkable amount of freedom to develop their potential.

They had a say over areas of school policy such as what subjects were available, including horticulture where the boys had the opportunity to plant vegetables in the school garden.[78]

In short, Pearse strived for the school to have more autonomy so it could reflect the uniqueness of the pupils and the locality.

St. Enda's mission statement was a quote from the Irish mythical hero, Cu Chulainn, exhorting pupils to follow a life of honour rather than materialism:

> " I care not though I were to live but one day and one night, provided my fame and deeds live after me."

Small classes

Pearse said the important thing in education was for children to discover their individual talents and for the teacher to help remove the barriers inhibiting the attainment of their full potential.

Class sizes were to be no more than 10 pupils, likened by Pearse to the teacher having a small group of disciples. He used this term to show the importance of dialogue in a child's development.[79]

According to the ethos of St. Enda's, children would eventually surpass the teacher in their learning, a view expressed by Plato, the Greek educationalist, who famously said he could not teach his students anything but could only help them to think.[80]

Pearse's philosophical views on education provide a strong foundation for its development in a New Ireland. His ideas for promoting learning would improve, in many ways, a current system that is quite exam driven.

Paulo Freire

We can see echoes of Pearse's views in the writings of Paulo Freire who wrote that young people should not be represented in education but should be encouraged to speak for themselves.[81]

Freire was arguing for a system that enabled students to be critical thinkers rather than taught to receive information.

St. Enda's boy's during a horticulture lesson in the school garden.
Image courtesy of the Pearse Museum Dublin.

The teacher would be working with the student on the same level, in dialogue, rather than coming across as having the 'superior knowledge'. Freire said:

> "It is in speaking their word that people, by naming the world, transform it. Dialogue imposes itself as the way by which they (the pupil) achieve significance as human beings."

A progressive education system would develop better within a confederal Ireland because it would arise from the people rather than being imposed by a central authority.

Integrated education

The main obstacles to building a New Ireland are the divisions among the people of Ireland as a whole.[82]

This problem is compounded by the system of religiously segregated education whereby most children from Protestant and Catholic backgrounds in Northern Ireland, attend religiously segregated schools.

It is indisputable that when children attend the same school, they have more opportunities to make friends with those from another tradition. Therefore, anyone interested in building a New Ireland should support a true form of integrated education.

Since the constitution of a New Ireland could be pluralist (separation of Church and state), no particular Church would be given a privileged position by the state in its provision of education.

Economic excellence in a New Ireland will be based upon an intensive development of the country's intellectual potential, so the higher education system will require massive investment.

With the development of better research skills, there will be more business innovation.

International schools

The establishment of international schools in Ireland could be a surprising success story because many students would be attracted from other countries by teaching them in their own language.[83]

Local and foreign students could pursue an academic career or go to a vocational university in applied sciences, but the great strength of the education system would be in its diversity.

For example: one option is that the people in a canton could decide how many teachers or other professionals are needed for the next 10 years.

Schools and third level colleges will provide the training for people to take up these positions, so skills shortages will not be a problem.

This policy has worked so well in Switzerland that paid employment for many young people is like just moving onto the next phase of their education.[84]

All pupils should get a healthy free school lunch every day because there may be quite a few who don't eat well at home.

There is no academic selection in the current Irish republic and their vocational schools at secondary level are open to all religious traditions.

Language

Language is an expression of power[85] and this is why imperialist powers sought to replace a native language with that of the colonist.

By speaking our language, we represent ourselves the way we understand that to be.

People who speak a language imposed upon them have been manipulated into expressing how they see the world through the language of someone else.

The Argentine educationalist, Paulo Freire, said:

> "The oppressed, having internalised the image of the oppressor and adapted his guidelines, are fearful of freedom."

Therefore, to speak one's native language is very fulfilling because we are reclaiming a unique awareness of self.

Hello Yassas

Gruetzi Hola

Sziastok Dia Duit

Salve Guten Tag

Hej Bonjour

Shalom Goddag

Dr. John Robb wrote:

"In the face of the contemporary challenge of nuclearism, gigantism and centralism, the potential of language and the images invoked by it, provides us with a powerful weapon with which to diminish the arrogance of others who might seek to control us."[86]

Synergy

The Irish language has the potential to spiritually renew Ireland by helping us to experience our own particular view of the world.

It should be encouraged and nurtured as a gift for all our diverse people but it would be foolish to impose it in any way.

Thomas Davis, the Young Irelander, makes a very convincing point that protecting a native language is the best way to safeguard the uniqueness of nationhood.[87] But diverse languages can also be advantageous to a country's development.

In Switzerland, Swiss German, French, Italian and Romanish are spoken. This diversity created a constructive tension whereby people from the disparate Alpine regions realised that if they were to survive, they needed to cooperate with each other.

This led to the growth of a consensual political tradition that probably would not have happened if there had been only one language spoken throughout all the regions.

The Swiss chose to respond in a positive way to cultural diverseness and it was the engine behind their famous ability to co-operate for the benefit of all.[88]

So unity can be created out of a variety of languages provided one language is not allowed to dominate another.

One could argue that there is now more equality between the various traditions in the North of Ireland, although there is still a way to go.

Progress made in eroding inequalities based upon religious and political affiliation has created the potential for further positive change.

We have a great opportunity now to make culture work for everyone, by being open to all languages.

Policing & Justice

A just and fair system of policing is built upon the consent of the people.

Where consent and consensus is lacking for structures of government, then major problems can arise around policing.

For every day policing and justice matters, an open, transparent and accountable police service is crucial otherwise it looses legitimacy among sections of the population.

In these circumstances, the police become a political arm of the state rather than being professionally objective from it.

A police service needs to be independent from party politics because in a democratic state, the judicial, executive and legislative functions should be separate.

Where this doesn't happen, it is unlikely that the police and the state it functions within will be sustainable.[89]

Accountable policing

In a divided society, a confederal political system is more inclined to produce accountable policing.

In Switzerland, each cantonal and municipal parliament has responsibility for policing its area.

The central confederal parliament has responsibilities regarding coordinated inter-cantonal police functions such as tackling organised drug trafficking and border security, in conjunction with the military.

Because sovereignty is vested in the people through the Swiss confederal system of political autonomies, the police service has the consent of the people.[90]

In this regard, the Swiss people are the police service and through having an excellent economy and education system, crime is very low and there is a sense of civic responsibility.

In a New Ireland, cantonal control of police and justice means that the police are under more democratic influences and this can only be a good thing. But any unfair practices could be dealt with at central confederal level.

The process of determining whether someone has committed a crime under the law is done through a professional system.

Innocence is assumed unless someone is proven guilty by the presentation and correct interpretation of all the evidence.

In a confederal Ireland, each county canton would have its own court and justice powers. There would be the opportunity for appeal to a higher confederal supreme court in Ireland.

As is the case in Switzerland, there would be an overall civil code to help harmonise inter-cantonal legal practice throughout the confederation.

Culture

The Swiss built a successful country, by harnessing the positivity of cultural diversity.

In Switzerland, like Ireland, the 2 main religions are Protestant and Catholic[91] but increasingly more people are identifying with no particular organised religion.

The situation in Ireland is more complex because a significant number of people in Northern Ireland identify with the UK and want to keep that constitutional link.

This means that Westminster has control over part of Ireland and this has been the underlying source of division in Northern Ireland.

Ultimately, it could be argued that these problems will ease when the constitutional question is resolved.

Switzerland came about because Alpine communities asked to join the growing Swiss confederation and this was partly to protect themselves from domination by outside forces. [92]

The country was formed as the result of a kind of voluntary coalition of mutual benefit.

But the history of Ireland is very different to Switzerland and it is easy to under estimate how the constitutional issue distorts things in Ireland.

Unity from diversity

Like in Ireland, the Swiss people have had conflict too and after a number of wars, they put their trust in arbitration and compromise.

The famous Swiss consensus rests upon a creative synergy and cleavage between their traditions of Protestant, Catholic, linguistic, urban and rural.

Grounded in their confederal system, ethno centralism or irredentist domination does not take hold.

A bigger role is given to smaller groups to the extent that diversity is a point of pride for the Swiss:

"The way the Swiss have created unity out of diversity is a central theme of their entire history. In this process, spanning many centuries, the individual characteristics of different regional and language groups were encouraged. Each made its own contribution to the common aim of greater harmony."

Swiss Made by R. James Breiding

Although we have a variety of cultural outlooks and loyalties in Ireland, diversity could be a means of creating social integration rather than division. The state should not take a cultural preference in language or any other expression of identity.

In the North, our constitutional views seem to direct much of our voting behaviour.[93]

A new conception of citizenship, reflected in the political institutions of Northern Ireland, would help to prevent tradition from becoming a source of strife and division.

A devolved assembly, linked to the UK but based upon accountability rather than identity, would recognise the unionist position.

But the seeds would be sown for the growth of a new future accommodation on the constitutional issue. This is because a civic administration in the North, over the years, would be building a shared future. It would be a situation preferable to the current system that reinforces community division.

A citizen- based approach to administration in the North of Ireland would buy time to enable each new generation to build a consensus on how they wish to view the constitutional question.

In a Northern Ireland context, the Swiss in their common sense and practical approach to politics, would not let differing constitutional views, prevent them from striking a sensible deal to live in the present.

Animal rights

In 1978, the Swiss animal welfare act was passed by 80% of the popular vote and in 1992, Switzerland was the first country to recognise the dignity of animals in its constitution.

The rights of animals should have strengthened safeguards within a New Ireland confederal constitution. People found guilty in a court of law of having purposely been cruel to animals should have custodial sentences that will act as a deterrent to others.

It is probably unrealistic to expect most people to be vegetarians but it is possible to encourage them to eat less meat.

I find the quote on opposite page from Buddha sums up the need to respect all life on our lovely planet:

"Once we experience and feel this interdependence of all living beings, we will cease to hurt, humiliate, exploit and kill another. We will want to free all sentient beings from suffering"

Buddha

A PATHWAY TO A NEW IRELAND

If we are to move forward as a society, then the hurt and suffering caused by the violence and injustice of the past will need to be eased by a truth for reconciliation process.

Much of the pain endured daily by victims of our conflict is made worse by falsehoods often perpetuated by the denial of truth. Dr. John Robb said that 'truth is the great weapon against falsehood.'

It is clear that for a healing process to happen, truth will need to be at its centre but not to cause more conflict by opening old wounds in a destructive way.

It may take many years before much of the truth is revealed behind the conflict in Northern Ireland, but, in the meantime, practical help should be given to surviving victims and their families.

Impartiality will be crucial and it would therefore be important to have an outside chairperson and body to manage the project.

Switzerland comes to mind, due to its esteemed record in facilitating dialogue to alleviate violent conflicts in our world.

Castlewellan forest park

Engagement

A challenge facing New Irelanders will be how to get the British and Irish governments to engage and to drive positive change.[94]

Westminster and the Dail parliaments usually ignore the problems of Northern Ireland until things get so bad that political solutions need to be found.

Because 2 jurisdictions exist in Ireland, it is easy to assume that it is just people in Northern Ireland who are divided, but in reality, this community division is an island wide phenomenon.

It is also a problem that needs to be addressed within the 'totality of relationships'[95] between these islands, the rest of Europe and the US.

Ireland's political problems are co-dependent in the sense that both states happened partly because of economic and political relationships throughout the whole island. And mainly because those who controlled the more industrial North wanted to off load the poorer, rural South.

It is therefore logical to argue that what happens outside both states will drive change within them.[96]

With divided peoples, peaceful politics is very important and eventually, change will happen, if those who seek it use their intellects and hearts to build a common ground.

Quite often, writers such as I use blueprints that could be implemented to manage change rather than looking at how to bring about change. But sometimes, outside circumstances can bring blue prints to life.

Eight steps to a Confederal Ireland

1. Healing – truth for reconciliation process
2. Local citizens conventions in North
3. Overall Northern Ireland citizen's convention
4. Referendum in Britain and the Irish Republic
5. Period of stability and confidence building
6. All island constitutional conference
7. Proposals for a New Ireland constitution put to the people North and South
8. Transition to a New Ireland economy to be underpinned by the US, Britain and Europe

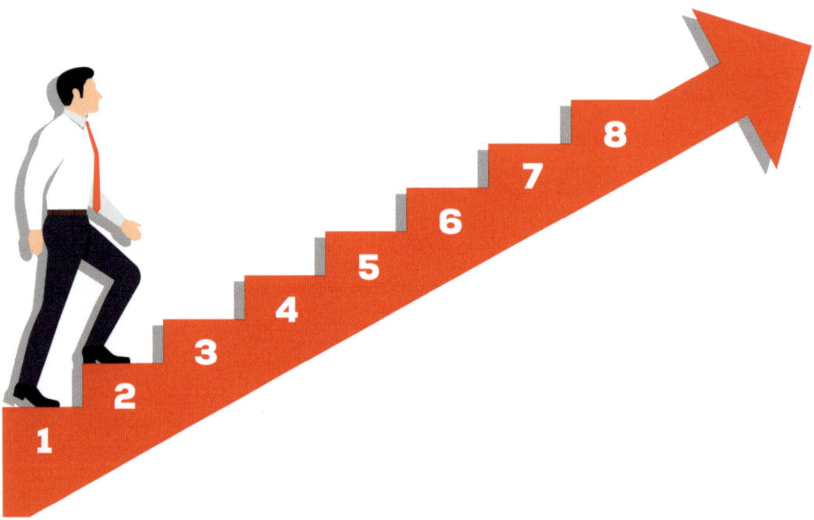

Self - confidence

Research carried out into various types of administration for the North might have the potential to move us forward politically.

These models may not be exclusive to Northern Ireland but could include other constitutional frameworks relating to the whole island and for Unionists on their relationship with the UK.

It would be better if the options presented encouraged Unionists to take part and this may only happen if they are limited to making the administration in Northern Ireland more accountable.

These possibilities could be presented for discussion at various local citizens conventions in Northern Ireland.[97]

Eventually, a multi-option pre-ferenda[98] may be used at each local convention, for people to vote in order of preference for their preferred model of government.

Once a consensus has been achieved at the local citizens conventions, an overall Northern citizens convention could be held, supported by the governments. It would have representatives from the individual citizens conventions, political parties and business community.

Participants at the Northern citizens convention would discuss the options from the local conventions

that had the most consensus and after some discussion, these options would be put to the people in the North for their vote in a pre-ferendum. [99]

Consensus

Through this method, consensus could be achieved and measured for the most popular form of government in Northern Ireland and this could start to move politics forward on a broad community basis.

This process should be underpinned by a joint declaration of support from the British, Irish, European and US governments.

Although this approach relies mainly upon citizen power, politicians, and political parties would have an important though not exclusive role to play.

Over the years and with new generations coming on board, there may eventually develop enough broad community agreement for a Northern constitutional convention that would elect people to take part in an all island convention.

This awareness among the broader population could start a process of agreement for a new constitution for the whole island but it would obviously need the consent of as many people as possible from both political traditions in the North.

If this agreement was not there, then those who were not happy with the proceedings could withdraw until such time that a foundation could be found to move forward again. It is very important that the whole community is at ease about things.[100]

Options for Northern Ireland

Power sharing

The disadvantage of power sharing is that it institutionalises sectarianism and does not focus upon accountability.

Ostensibly it would seem that power sharing has been tried in Northern Ireland with the Good Friday-Belfast Agreement in 1998. But after the St. Andrews Agreement of 2006, there was a local power carve-up between the 2 largest political parties.[101]

Since August 15th 1998, political violence in Northern Ireland has not been so intensely prolonged and it is important to recognise that injustice is violence too.

But there was a failure to bring about good administration for the province, with scandals arising from the alleged misuse of public money.

Thankfully it can be said that the relative absence of

political violence has meant community relations were not as bad as during the conflict between 1969-1998.

Voluntary coalition

This is a system for those parties that want to form a government and who agree a program of administration before taking part in an executive.

It would mean that the smaller parties could go ahead and form an administration while the larger ones would have the choice of going into 'opposition'.

There would be a system of weighted voting whereby no major decisions could be made without over 65% support from all the parties in the administration.

My main criticism of this option is that it doesn't improve upon the accountability problem in the previous power sharing arrangement.[102]

Direct accountability model

This is my own model that I have developed for the following reasons: it focuses on building a more accountable administration rather than cementing community divisions.

The premise underpinning the direct accountability model is that it dispenses with the need to share power between politicians and instead shares it with the people.

If the administration at Stormont and throughout the province is more accountable, there will be fewer opportunities for the abuse of devolved power. Hence power sharing is not necessary and we can move closer to a more shared society.[103]

Political circle idea

It was designed by a friend and consists of a circle numbering 60 to 100 people who sit in an assembly.

They are equal and paid the same salary. At this round table, 7 people will have responsibility for all government departments. They must reflect the overall 70% + consensus of the rest of the assembly.

The assembly nominates these 7 people and there are no political parties. People are elected to the assembly by general vote from names put forward for election from citizen's assemblies.[104]

Direct rule

This type of administration is really a holding mechanism until a provincial assembly can be formed.

It does not lay the basis for more accountable

government and hinders the political self-confidence that is needed in Northern Ireland to advance to a new political framework.

Direct rule keeps some basic services and jobs functioning but to a very limited and unsatisfactory level.[105]

Joint authority

A form of joint authority happened within the Anglo Irish Agreement process and it was a precursor to the Belfast – Good Friday Agreement (1998).

It's a fairly arbitrary way to do administration because it is remote and not based upon political consensus. Its viewed in certain quarters as an emergency measure until a form of devolved government can be established in Northern Ireland.[106]

Direct accountability model in detail

The direct accountability model is very straightforward: the subvention money from the treasury in London would be fairly distributed to each county in the North according to population and needs.

An equality and finance body, that would replace the department of finance at Stormont, would implement safeguards to ensure equality of access to resources.

For example: by using this model, fewer people could argue that their local hospital is being treated unfairly because power would no longer reside with the department of health over the distribution of money.

Finance allocated to a small acute hospital would be calculated according to the direct accountability resources formula. A health care forum in a local hospital would be given its fair share of money according to its population and it would have control over how this money is spent.

A leaner department of health means less red tape, freeing resources for frontline services.

Political parties, ministers and senior civil servants would thus, hopefully, be less likely to make unaccountable decisions to close smaller hospitals without the consent of local people.

Cantons in Northern Ireland would be an important part of the direct accountability model and they may be a useful way to build up community self-confidence.

Maybe a more practical way to progress this would be for our local councils to become cantons,[107] but implementing a system of direct democracy in conjunction with towns and townlands that could be municipalities.

Although these cantons would not exercise the sovereignty of a canton within a confederal Ireland, they could represent considerable progress in making administration in the North more accountable.

Many in the Irish republic are not aware of the benefits of a confederal system, so a first step might be to make an aspect of it work in the North. Hopefully their success would encourage the people of Southern Ireland to move toward a confederal system.

The challenge is how can the conditions be created so the British government will initiate this process of citizen involvement in setting up a more accountable administration in the North?

It would be important for citizens to first be aware of their power, then to contest elections and win enough support to exert influence on the governments.

This could be a short-term or long-term project, depending upon how hungry people are for change but soil cultivated now could bear fruit in the future.

"Why not spend less time dwelling upon carving up power between religious blocks and focus upon how to make the Stormont administration more accountable. An element of direct democracy could be included, giving the public a say in decision-making at a local and provincial level"[108]

The Author

Your future poll

It could be very probable that the unqualified use of self-determination in Ireland to underwrite one tradition majoritarianism through a border poll, might lead to conflict and violence.

The solution to this problem is that self-determination should be qualified by the need to achieve consensus. [109]

Sometime in the more distant future, the British government could call for Northern Ireland what is commonly known as a border poll.

But what options will it present to the public? Would such a poll ask the question 'Do you want to remain in the UK or become part of a United Ireland?'

In a border poll, it would make more sense to give the public a list of possible constitutional options to consent to in order of preference.

These could include remaining within the UK or supporting a confederal Ireland but the crucial point is that consensus would be achieved rather than the unrest that could happen from a slim, one tradition majoritarian vote for departition.

A
B
1
3
C
D
4
2

A possible your future poll ballot paper

Please number in order of preference:

☐ Confederal Ireland outside the UK

☐ Federal Ireland outside the UK

☐ Northern Ireland to remain in the UK

☐ Centralised Ireland outside the UK

Consensus for a form of government would be infinitely preferable even to a situation where a majority among all traditions (parallel consent) voted for a united Ireland but did not know what form it should have.

The worse case scenario would be where 50% plus 1 voted to end partition, leaving over half the population of Northern Ireland alienated. It's the people that need united, not the territory.

The shambolic Brexit referendum clearly illustrates what can happen if things are not properly thought through.

With a vision of the future based upon the consensus of the people from the whole community, north and south, there is more chance of achieving a successful outcome and avoiding conflict.

A great challenge arises from the existence of two jurisdictions on the island of Ireland, controlled by very centralised powers. If there was a narrow majority for unity but no wider community consensus for it and its form, a unionist minority may wish to secede from an all-Ireland future, leading to repartition.

Therefore, why not replace the term 'border poll' with a 'your future poll' where people can vote for a series of options and arrive at a consensus.

There would need to be at least a year of awareness building on what the various constitutional options mean before a 'Your Future Poll' could happen.

A united people and better society in Ireland will not happen until the hardest border of all is addressed: the divided community.

> "In today's global village-secession is a contradiction in terms. Independence is not valid outside of a relationship of interdependence."
>
> Dr. John Robb

Ireland & Switzerland

It can be unwise to compare the histories of two countries due to their individual circumstances but such comparisons give valuable insights.

The high point of civilisation in Ireland was undoubtedly from the 5th to 9th centuries, when the great Christian monasteries were at the peak of their development. [110]

This was partly due to their semi-autonomous relationship with Rome, a freedom from centralised control that fostered a creativity unsurpassed in Ireland before or since.

Irish monks from Bangor abbey in Ireland brought their Christian message to people in the dense forest regions of central Europe.

One of these monks was called Gall and he established a hermitage in the Alps that became an abbey, town and eventually the canton of St. Gallen in modern day Switzerland. [111]

The Bangor monks transcribed ancient texts that can be seen today in the Swiss abbey library of St. Gall, conserving much of the world's learning for future generations. Kept safe in the abbey of Gallon, these manuscripts were protected from Viking raids in Ireland.[112]

St. Gall and the Bear

Ireland's influence

"Switzerland owes much of its development to Ireland"

The Author

It could be argued the Swiss confederal system cannot be adapted to Ireland because both countries are different. This presupposes the Swiss are ahead of the people of Ireland about how to organise their country.

But the contribution of Irish monks to Swiss culture shows the very positive influence of Ireland upon Switzerland and that both nations have long established cultural connections.

A legend arose in the Swiss Alps, about a wild bear charging Gall's camp-fire at night but was stopped in its tracks by the monk's presence.

The bear went back into the forest and returned with wood for Gall's fire becoming his loyal friend.[113]

The reason I am telling this story is to show the historic bonds between Ireland and Switzerland, highlighting the important point that Switzerland owes much of its development to Ireland.

If a confederation is established in Ireland, we are not importing an alien idea but renewing our historic links with the Swiss.

Civilisation

Thomas Cahill wrote in: *How the Irish Saved Civilisation*:

"Without the mission of the Irish monks, who single handedly re-founded European civilisation throughout the continent in the bays and valleys of their exile, the world that came after them would have been an entirely different one. A world without books and our own world would never come to be."

I included this quote to show the wonderful culture of learning in Ireland many centuries ago, as a benchmark for what could be achieved here again.

But it would be repetitive to give a narrative of the country's history in this little publication.

You can read Ireland's story in other books but basically, with a few exceptional individuals, it was all down hill, as a society, after the decline of the old monasteries. The conquest of Ireland then became almost intractable.[114]

It is true that the overall standard of living has increased for the masses in modern Ireland but without political autonomy, it is very difficult to become an advanced civilisation, breaking new ground in research for the common good.

Where does this leave us today?

John Mitchel, the Young Irelander, argued that the development of society is circular, not linear. He meant that countries do not usually progress from a low point and over many centuries, become an advanced civilisation and then stabilise.

Mitchel's theory is that a country's development can be circular, becoming an advanced civilisation, followed by a period of decline,[115] which is what happened in Ireland.

Gandhi was once asked by a journalist what he thought of western civilisation and Gandhi responded: 'I think it would be a good idea', meaning that western powers were not civilised.[116]

Experience of democracy

In Ireland, we have certainly progressed as a society in some respects but we haven't reached that point of development that we are capable of reaching.

A challenge and an opportunity for the people of Ireland to make democratic, economic and societal progress is our limited experience of democracy and self-government.

From the downfall of the advanced monastic system and the arrival of the Normans in Ireland in 1169, there was a period of over 749 years before the first Dail was elected in Ireland by universal franchise. [117]

After the Anglo Irish treaty of 1921, there was a very limited representative democracy in the Irish republic and virtually a one party state in the North up to 1972.

There has been an on-off assembly in Northern Ireland up until recently.

The old Swiss direct democracy was happening hundreds of years before the French revolution of 1789. It prepared the ground for the development of the Swiss confederation. [118]

It could be argued that Ireland's experience of democracy of any kind has really only happened over the last 96 years. Compare this with Switzerland and we can see why their democracy became one of the most advanced in the world while Ireland's is diluted and centralised in Brussels, Dublin and London.

Multi-nationals

The southern part of Ireland's economy is partly dependent upon US multi-national investment and EU – IMF handouts.[119]

Although the Irish republic's economy gives prosperity to a few, it does not have one of the main characteristics of a civilisation: self-determination based upon consensus. This is because the EU has a dominant influence in Southern Ireland's affairs.

The Swiss were able to utilise their unique circumstances and history for their overall benefit whereas the people of Ireland were not as flexible when trying to make progress.

Although it is an unfair comparison, because in Ireland, the colonial oppression was more insurmountable than what pertained for the Swiss Alpine communities. Yet there is much we can learn from the Swiss.

Because Ireland is an island, it was more secluded from European progressive political influences, despite the Irish Gaelic system being very advanced and even democratic in certain respects.

Civic way

The conquest of the Irish people is unlikely to have anything to do with the Gaelic temperament being more volatile than the Swiss. We are all made of flesh and blood, human beings inclined to react in a similar way when affected by our environment.

The seeds of downfall were sown in the failure to modernise politically and thus match the power of the state used so effectively by the English ruling class to defeat the Gaelic leaders at the end of the 16th century.[120]

It was a weakness that led to the eventual conquest of Ireland. The writer, Sean O'Faolain, put it like this:

"What they lacked (the Irish) was something inherent in their system of life, a lack which made the English call them uncivilised; to wit-government."[121]

It could be less likely such a criticism is levelled in the future if we adapt a considered and more methodical approach to alleviating divisions that exist among the people of this beautiful island.

This would include a civic way, by stimulating more discussion and awareness about what is better government and how to achieve it through peace, reconciliation and consensus politics.

The creativity of the citizen should be encouraged to consider solutions to old problems and the people should be given a direct influence at the negotiating places for a New Ireland.

Political parties and politicians will have their role to play in this but their influence should not dominate that of the citizen.

It is important to remember what the Swiss 18th century political thinker, Jean Jacques Rousseau said:

"The moment a people gives itself to representatives, it is no longer free."

CONCLUSION

The question has been posed by a unionist politician, 'where is the evidence that unionists will be respected in a united Ireland?' [122]

Anyone calling for a New Ireland should take very seriously unionist concerns about what it would mean for them.

Further research is required not only into what forms of government a New Ireland could have but more importantly, how can a process be developed to build confidence for it.

We trust each other usually by past behaviour and this can be sometimes a precedent for how we will be treated in the future.[123] How can this trust and confidence be strengthened in those who feel most reluctant to support a united Ireland?

The establishment of a new more accountable form of administration in Northern Ireland might help, if this is possible.

We could build a better society in the North by co-operating with each other, the Irish republic, EU, US and London.

In this way trust could be developed for discussions to take place on a broad community basis for a New Ireland.

It may take generations or it could happen a lot quicker but life is full of positive possibilities.

Endnotes

1 BBC news reports - March 2020
2 *A Blue Print for Survival* (Pub.1972)
3 Visualising a New Ireland seminar at the Canal Court Hotel Newry 2016
4 RTE broadcasts at the time
5 Conversation with the Beat Loeliger - Swiss ambassador to Dublin
6 Ditto
7 Writings of Dr. John Robb - Irish Senator - founder of the New Ireland Group
8 Writings of Peter Emerson
9 Swiss information website
10 Ditto
11 Visualising a New Ireland seminar, Canal Court Hotel, Newry, 2016
12 Discussion at meeting of New Ireland Group
13 Writings of Dr. John Robb
14 Ditto
15 *Free and Swiss: the story of Switzerland* by Georg Thurer (pub: 1948)
16 Writings of Dr. John Robb
17 SDLP press statements
18 Ibid
19 Eire Nua document - Linen Hall Library Belfast
20 Conversations with business experts
21 Stormont Department of Finance data
22 Irish republic's Department of Health data
23 Conversations with Dr. Stan Papenfus - Pychologist
24 Publications by the New Ireland Group
25 Conversations with business expert
26 Press statements by Irish government officials
27 Conversation for work colleague
28 Writings of Dr. John Robb
29 Irish News newspaper report
30 RTE media reports
31 Official statements at the time from the Irish government
32 Press statements by SDLP leader John Hume
33 BBC media coverage of the Yellow Vest protests
34 Northern Ireland Electoral Commission voting data
35 *Hitler* by Joachim C. Fest (Pub.1973)

36 *A Blood Red Autumn: Thomas Russell and the Irish rising of 1803* by Francis Gallagher (Pub. 2003)
37 Swiss Review magazine
38 Writings of Dr. John Robb
39 Media coverage of 2018 Irish presidential election
40 Friend in the business community
41 Political writings of Karl Marx
42 Ibid
43 *Swiss Made: the untold story behind Switzerland's success* (Pub. 2013) by R. James Breiding
44 Ditto
45 Ditto
46 Research into the Economy of the Irish republic
47 Visualising a New Ireland conference - Canal Court Hotel-Newry-2016
48 *Ireland Yesterday and Tomorrow* by Bulmer Hobson (Pub:1968)
49 *A Blueprint for Survival* (Pub: 1972)
50 Ditto
51 *Dueling Dragons* by Marjorie Harshaw Robie - speech by John Martin in House of Commons
52 Walks in Down District and Camlough countryside
53 EU subsidy payments data on Google
54 Swiss information website
55 Ditto
56 See Swiss constitution on New Ireland Vision website
57 Talk at Newry on Marine life in Carlingford Lough
58 Mourne Observer newspaper 2019 - articles on local fishing and Brexit
59 BBC media coverage
60 Discussions with public service employees
61 Discussion with Dr. Stan Papenfus - Psychologist
62 Ditto
63 Richard Branson - autobiography
64 *Book of Newry* by Michael Mc Keown (Pub: 2008)
65 History of the Federal Reserve DVD
66 Google data
67 Conference on Roger Casement - Newcastle, Co. Down
68 *Free and Swiss: the story of Switzerland* by Georg Thurer (Pub: 1948)
69 Media reports and Department of Health staffing data
70 Google data

71 Writings of Dr. John Robb
72 Ditto
73 Ibid
74 *Long live the small acute hospital* by Dr. John Robb
75 Ditto
76 Meeting with Teresita Trujillo (2012) Cuban Ambassador to Dublin. Meeting with Hugo Ramos, 2018, Cuban Ambassador to Dublin.
77 Presentation about St. Enda's school by a representative from the Pearse Museum Dublin and delivered at Newry museum, (2016).
78 Ditto
79 *The murder machine* by Patrick Pearse
80 Conversation with Dr. Stan Papenfus - psychologist
81 *Pedagogy of the oppressed* by Paulo Freire (Pub: 1968)
82 Media statements by John Hume - MP, MEP and former leader of the Northern Ireland Social Democratic and Labour Party (SDLP)
83 *Swiss made*
84 Ditto
85 David Hammond reference in an article by Dr. John Robb: 'Language: local and global' published in the Mourne Echo newspaper, August 2000.
86 Mourne Echo newspaper, August 2000 Edition
87 Writings of Thomas Davis, Young Irelander
88 Free and Swiss by Georg Thurer
89 Discussions on policing organised by the New Ireland Group
90 Swiss information website
91 *Free and Swiss*
92 Ditto
93 Opinion of media commentators and electoral data
94 Contribution from the audience at a Killough (Co. Down) summer school on Ireland's future
95 Media statements by John Hume MP and MEP
96 Discussions at UCAN group meetings, Downpatrick
97 Citizen's convention organised by the New Ireland Group and held at Queens University Belfast in the 1980s.
98 New Ireland Group
99 Ditto and writings of Dr. John Robb
100 *A Shared Homeplace* by Seamus Mallon with Andy Pollak (Pub: 2019)
101 Press coverage of the Northern Ireland Assembly
102 Google search

103 My own model of administration influenced by the writings of Dr. John Robb, the Swiss system
104 This idea was developed at UCAN community group meetings at Downpatrick and the founder of that group.
105 Analysis in provincial newspapers over the years
106 Ditto
107 Conversations with Newry businessman
108 My own quote
109 Writings of Dr. John Robb
110 *How the Irish saved civilisation* by Thomas Cahill
111 *Free and Swiss*
112 Ditto
113 Google and *Free and Swiss*
114 Extensive reading on the history of Ireland
115 Political writings and letters of John Mitchel - Young Irelander
116 Old BBC news reel covering Gandhi's visit
117 Extensive reading on the history of Ireland
118 *Free and Swiss*
119 Media broadcasts about fall of the Celtic Tiger economy
120 *The Great O'Neill* by Sean O' Faolain
121 Ditto
122 Question was posed by a Unionist politician
123 Conversations with Dr. Stan Papenfus-psychologist